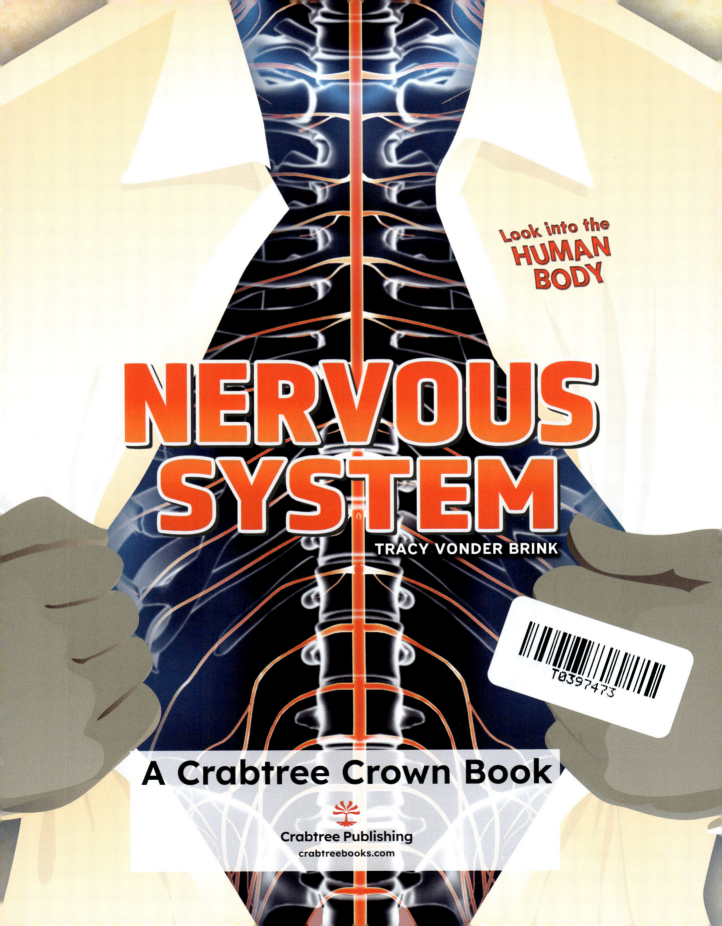

Look into the HUMAN BODY

NERVOUS SYSTEM

TRACY VONDER BRINK

A Crabtree Crown Book

Crabtree Publishing
crabtreebooks.com

School-to-Home Support for Caregivers and Teachers

This appealing book is designed to teach students about core subject areas. Students will build upon what they already know about the subject, and engage in topics that they want to learn more about. Here are a few guiding questions to help readers build their comprehension skills. Possible answers appear here in red.

Before Reading:

What do I know about the nervous system?

- I know the nervous system is part of my body.
- I know my brain is part of my nervous system.

What do I want to learn about this topic?

- I want to know how the nervous system works.
- I want to learn about the parts of the nervous system.

During Reading:

I'm curious to know...

- I'm curious to know how my brain sends signals to my body.
- I'm curious to know the difference between the voluntary and the involuntary nervous system.

How is this like something I already know?

- I know my brain controls my body.
- I know I have both a voluntary and an involuntary nervous system.

After Reading:

What was the author trying to teach me?

- The author was trying to teach me what my nervous system does.
- The author was trying to teach me how my brain sends out signals.

How did the images and captions help me understand more?

- The images helped me understand how the parts of the nervous system work together.
- The captions gave me extra information about each part of the nervous system.

TABLE OF CONTENTS

CHAPTER 1
Meet Your Body................................. 4

CHAPTER 2
Your Nervous System........................... 7

CHAPTER 3
Your Brain, Spinal Cord, and Nerves.............. 10

CHAPTER 4
Your Nervous System at Work....................16

CHAPTER 5
Nervous System Problems...................... 20

CHAPTER 6
Taking Care of Your Nervous System.............. 26

GLOSSARY.. 30

INDEX...31

COMPREHENSION QUESTIONS 31

ABOUT THE AUTHOR 32

CHAPTER 1
MEET YOUR BODY

Have you ever wondered how your body takes in air, moves your blood, digests your lunch, and reads this book...all at the same time? It begins with cells.

A cell is the basic unit of life. Cells are sometimes called "the building blocks of life." You are made up of trillions of cells! Different cells have different kinds of jobs. For example, nerve cells carry messages between your brain and your body. The human body has around 200 different kinds of cells.

Body Basics

Every living thing is made up of cells. Cells can't be seen with the eyes alone. Up to 10,000 human cells could fit on the head of a pin.

Your body has many different **structures** made of cells. Your brain is one of these structures. Different structures make up body systems. Each system has important tasks. The structures in a system work together to keep your body running.

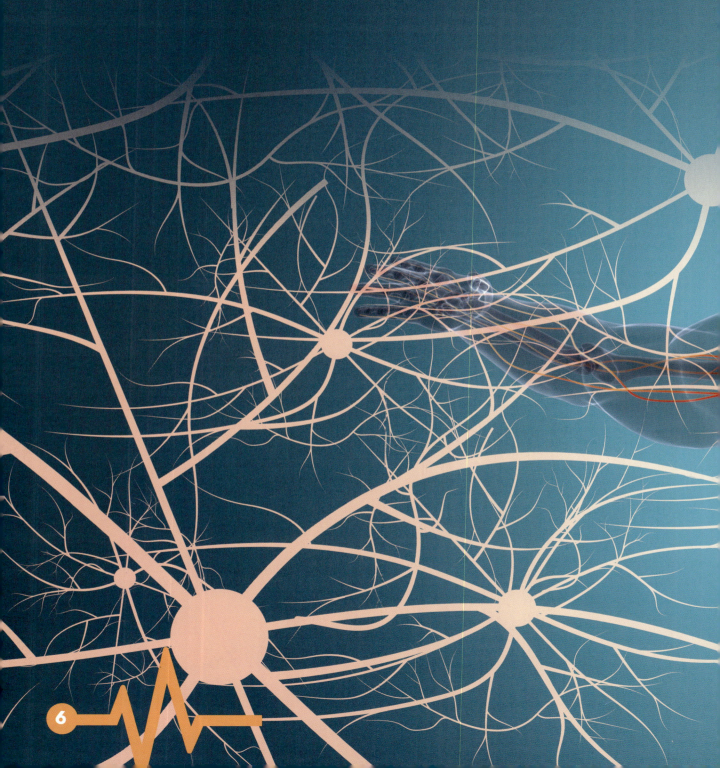

CHAPTER 2
YOUR NERVOUS SYSTEM

The nervous system is your body's control center. It **regulates** everything your body does. Your nervous system also helps your body react to changes. It has two main parts: the central nervous system and the peripheral nervous system.

All animals with a backbone have a central nervous system and a peripheral nervous system.

THE CENTRAL NERVOUS SYSTEM

The brain and the spinal cord make up the central nervous system (CNS). The CNS gathers information from the whole body. It sends out signals that tells your muscles what to do. For example, if you clap, the CNS signals the muscles that move your arms and hands.

THE PERIPHERAL NERVOUS SYSTEM

The peripheral nervous system (PNS) branches out from your brain and spinal cord. The PNS is made up of **nerves**. The PNS helps your body communicate with itself. It also helps control actions you don't think about, such as your heart beating.

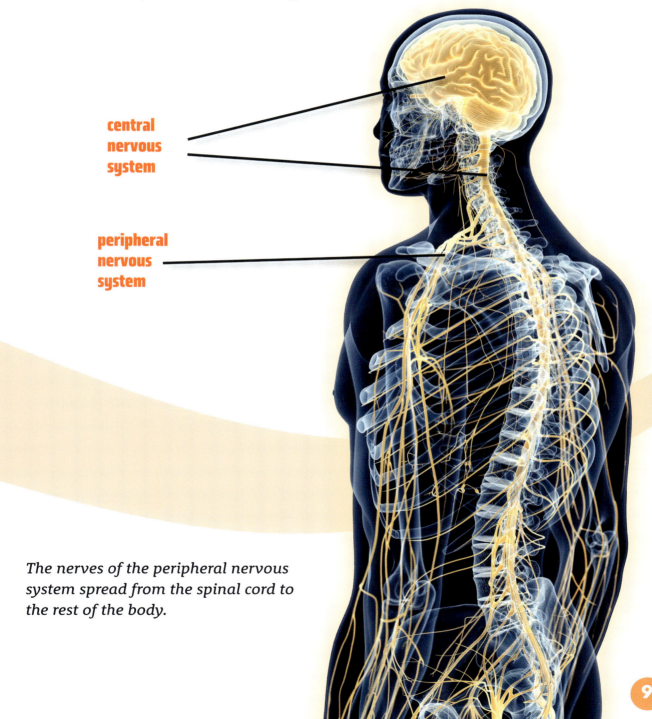

The nerves of the peripheral nervous system spread from the spinal cord to the rest of the body.

CHAPTER 3

YOUR BRAIN, SPINAL CORD, AND NERVES

Your brain is your body's control room and super computer. The largest section of the brain is called the cerebrum. The cerebrum is the part that understands information gathered by your senses. It allows you to think, talk, and much more. It also plays a part in controlling and **processing** feelings and memories.

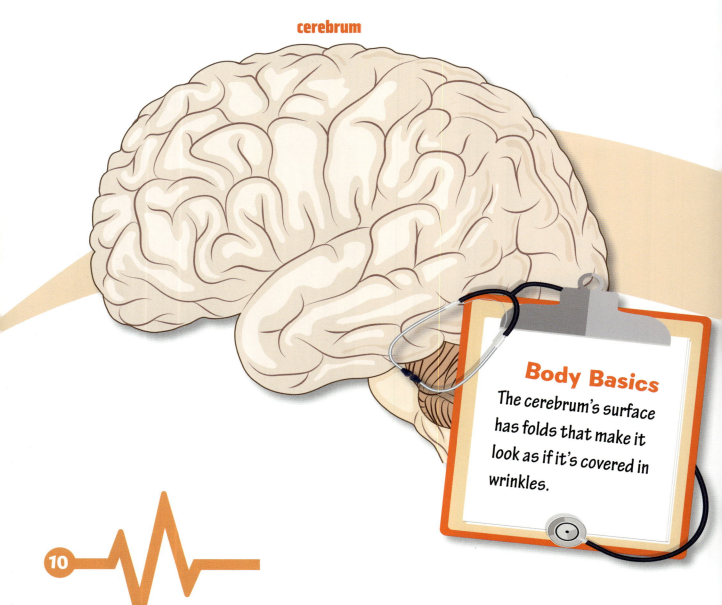

cerebrum

Body Basics
The cerebrum's surface has folds that make it look as if it's covered in wrinkles.

The cerebrum has two sides, called hemispheres. The right hemisphere controls the left side of your body. The right hemisphere helps you be creative. The left hemisphere controls your body's right side. The left hemisphere is what helps you write, do math, and understand what you learn.

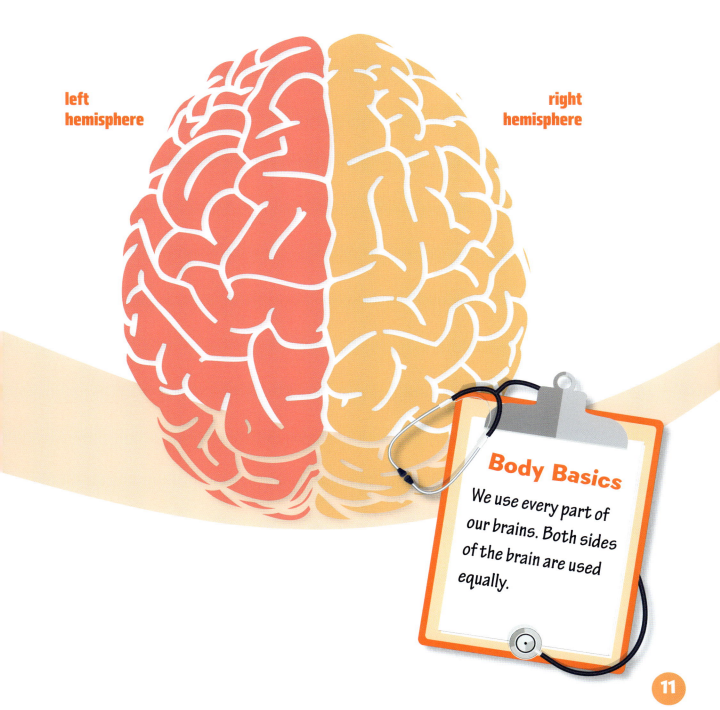

left hemisphere

right hemisphere

Body Basics

We use every part of our brains. Both sides of the brain are used equally.

The cerebellum is below the cerebrum. It controls your **balance** and some of your muscles. The brainstem is underneath the cerebellum. The brainstem connects the rest of the brain to the spinal cord. The brainstem regulates your heartbeat, breathing, and many other things your body does **automatically**.

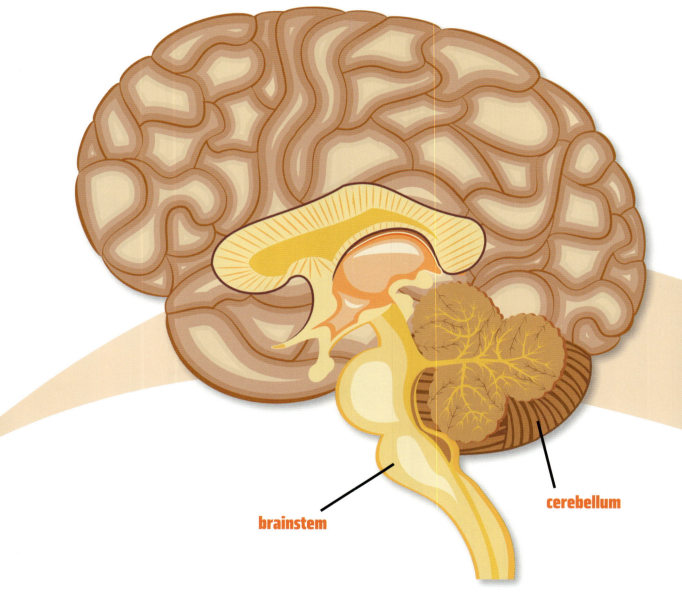

An adult human brain weighs about three pounds (1,300 to 1,400 grams).

YOUR SPINAL CORD

The spinal cord is like a cable that connects your body and brain. It is made of nerve **fibers** and runs from your brainstem down your spine. Messages from your body go up the spinal cord to the brain. Commands from your brain travel down the spinal cord to your body.

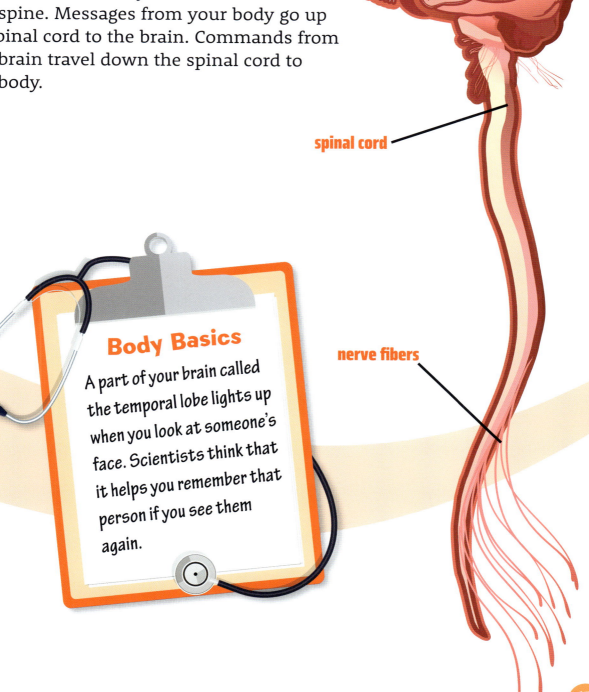

spinal cord

nerve fibers

Body Basics

A part of your brain called the temporal lobe lights up when you look at someone's face. Scientists think that it helps you remember that person if you see them again.

YOUR NERVES

Nerves are like a network that constantly carry signals back and forth between your body and your brain. Nerves are made up of nerve cells called neurons. Information travels along neurons as electrical or **chemical** signals.

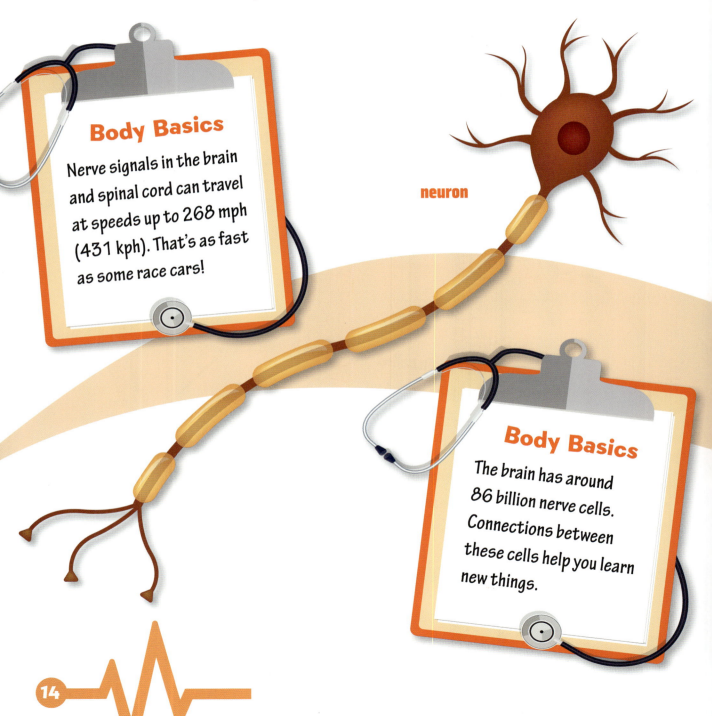

neuron

Body Basics

Nerve signals in the brain and spinal cord can travel at speeds up to 268 mph (431 kph). That's as fast as some race cars!

Body Basics

The brain has around 86 billion nerve cells. Connections between these cells help you learn new things.

Different nerves carry different kinds of messages. For example, sensory nerves send information from your skin, eyes, and ears to your brain. Motor nerves carry commands from your brain to your muscles.

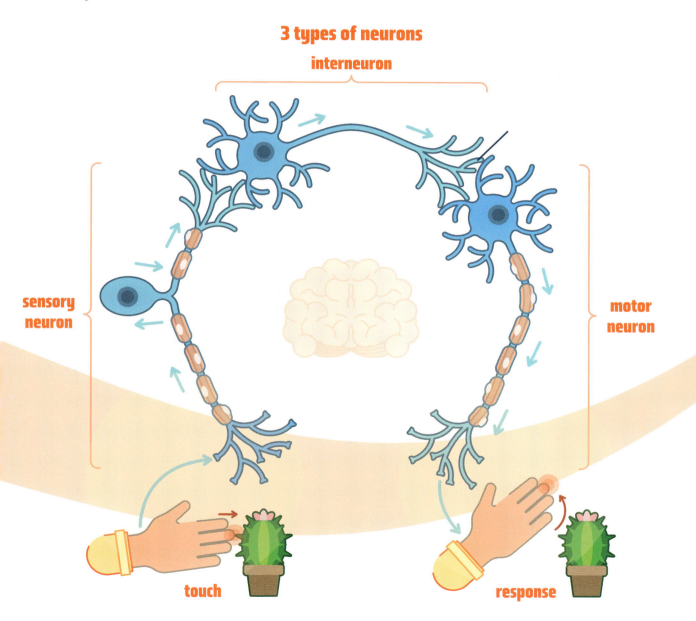

Interneurons are nerve cells that help transfer signals between sensory and motor nerves.

CHAPTER 4:
YOUR NERVOUS SYSTEM AT WORK
VOLUNTARY NERVOUS SYSTEM

Take a deep breath. Hold it a moment, then let it out. You just used your voluntary nervous system! When you decided to take that deep breath, your brain told your lungs to breathe in longer than usual. You use your voluntary nervous system whenever you decide to move your body. Any action we choose to do is called voluntary.

INVOLUNTARY NERVOUS SYSTEM

Your involuntary nervous system is what allows your body to work automatically. You breathe in and out all day, every day, without having to think about it. The involuntary nervous system is in charge any time your body works or reacts on its own. It's called involuntary because we don't think to control it.

Body Basics

Does your heart beat faster when you're scared? That's your involuntary nervous system at work. It's giving you more energy in case you need to run away.

REFLEXES

A reflex is your body's involuntary reaction to something. Some reflexes help keep you safe. For example, if you accidentally touch a hot stove, your reflexes quickly pull your hand away before you're badly burned.

Body Basics

Sneezing is also a reflex. You sneeze when something, such as dust, irritates your nose. Sneezing helps clear it out.

Your voluntary and involuntary nervous systems are both part of your peripheral nervous system. They're always at work, carrying signals between your brain and the rest of your body.

A cough is your body's involuntary response to an irritation in your throat or lungs.

CHAPTER 5
NERVOUS SYSTEM PROBLEMS
BRAIN INJURIES

The skull protects the brain, but sometimes severe accidents can cause a brain injury. Harm to the brain can kill nerve cells. Dead or damaged nerve cells can no longer send signals. People who suffer severe brain damage may have trouble thinking, speaking, or moving.

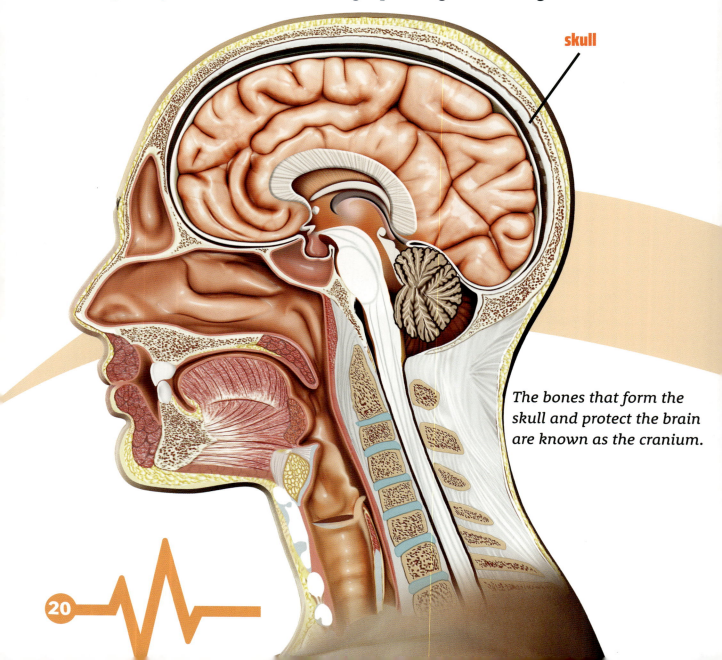

skull

The bones that form the skull and protect the brain are known as the cranium.

SPINAL CORD INJURIES

A broken neck can injure the spinal cord. If the spinal cord is damaged, it can no longer carry messages to and from the brain. People with spinal cord injuries may be **paralyzed**.

Body Basics

Injured skin and bones can regrow, but the nerves in the brain can't. An injured brain cannot heal itself.

21

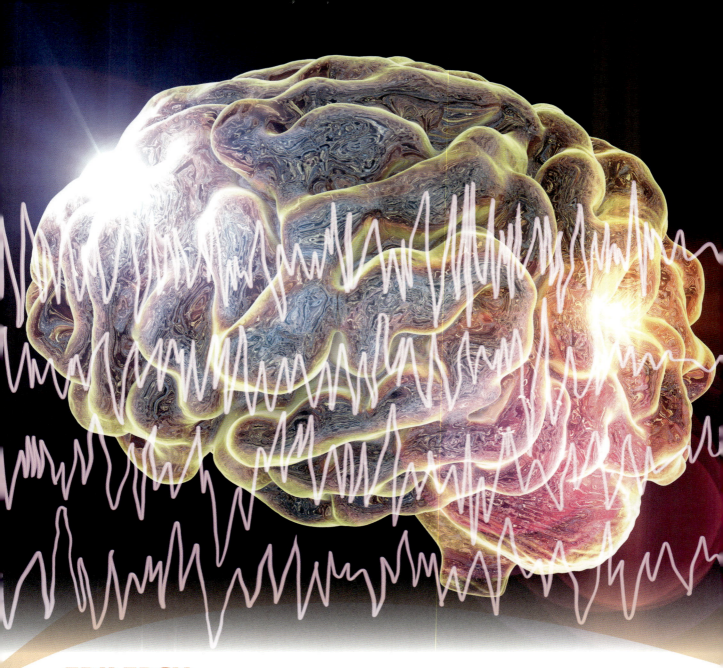

EPILEPSY

Some people are born with or develop conditions that affect how the nervous system works. Epilepsy is a condition that causes the brain to send out too many signals at the wrong time. This causes the body to have **seizures**.

CEREBRAL PALSY

Cerebral palsy is a condition in which the brain doesn't send enough signals. Some people with cerebral palsy are unable to walk. Some people are born with cerebral palsy. Others develop the condition after an injury.

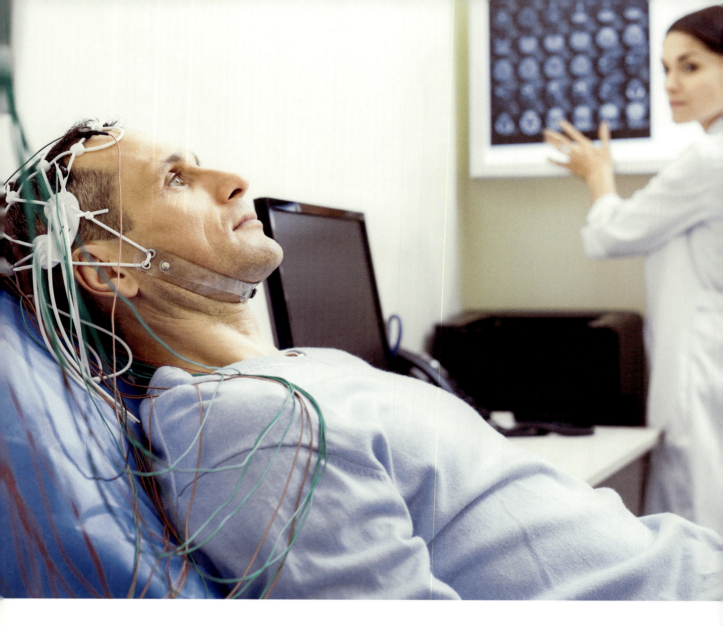

HOW DOCTORS HELP

Doctors use special equipment to check the nervous system when things go wrong. An EEG test measures the brain's electrical signals. An MRI scan makes images of the brain or spinal cord. These tests help doctors decide on a treatment.

During an EEG, sensors placed on the head detect the brain's electrical activity.

Some conditions, such as epilepsy, may be helped with medication. People who struggle to walk may use braces, crutches, or a wheelchair. Service dogs help some. For example, a service dog can be trained to open doors, turn on lights, or sense when the person needs help.

CHAPTER 6
TAKING CARE OF YOUR NERVOUS SYSTEM
EAT, DRINK, AND SLEEP WELL

Eating healthy foods keeps your nervous system in good shape. Foods with protein, such as meat, fish, and eggs, help build brain tissue. Drinking plenty of water and sleeping 9 to 12 hours every night also keeps your brain running at its best.

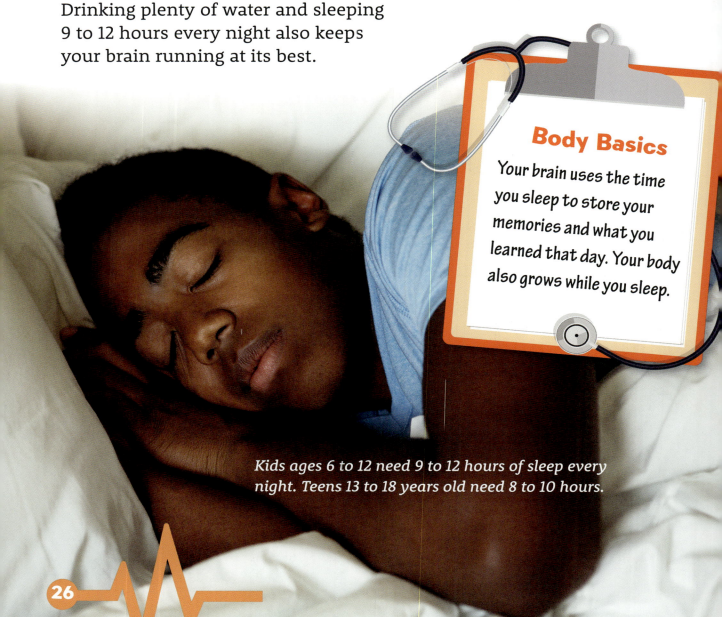

Body Basics
Your brain uses the time you sleep to store your memories and what you learned that day. Your body also grows while you sleep.

Kids ages 6 to 12 need 9 to 12 hours of sleep every night. Teens 13 to 18 years old need 8 to 10 hours.

SEE YOUR DOCTOR

Regular checkups help keep you healthy. Your doctor can make sure you're growing well. **Immunizations** protect you from diseases that might hurt your nervous system.

WEAR SAFETY GEAR

Wearing a helmet is one of the best things you can do for your brain. A helmet helps protect your head from a fall off your bike or an injury during sports. Always wear your seat belt in a car. It keeps you safer in a crash.

Talking to friends, playing a game, or throwing a ball for your dog—your nervous system helps you do it all. Take good care of it, and it will keep you going!

GLOSSARY

automatically (ah-tuh-MA-tuh-klee): Done without thinking about it

balance (BAL-uhns): The ability to keep the body steady without falling down

chemical (KEH-muh-kl): Made by processes that involve changes to atoms or molecules

fiber (FAI-br): Threadlike parts that form the tissues of animals and plants

immunization (i-myoo-nuh-ZAY-shn): Protecting a person from a disease by giving them an injection of a vaccine

nerves (NURVZ): Bundles of cells that carry carry messages to and from the brain and body

paralyzed (PEH-ruh-lized): The loss of the ability to move or feel in a part of the body

processing (PROS-es-iz): Changing or preparing using a series of steps or actions

regulate (REH-gyuh-layt): To adjust the amount or rate of something

structure (STRUHK-chr): Something made of many parts arranged together

seizures (SEE-zhrz): Sudden shaking movements of the body that cannot be controlled

INDEX

brain 5-6, 8-16, 19-24, 26, 28

cell 4-6, 14-15, 20

cerebral palsy 23

cerebrum 10-12

cerebellum 12

epilepsy 22, 25

nerve fibers 13

nerves 4, 9-10, 13-15, 20–21

neurons 14-15

spinal cord 8-10, 12-14, 21, 24

COMPREHENSION QUESTIONS

1. What are sometimes called the building blocks of life?
   a. nerves
   b. reflexes
   c. cells

2. The brain and the spinal cord make up the _____ nervous system.
   a. peripheral
   b. central
   c. reflex

3. Your heart beating automatically is part of the _____ nervous system.
   a. involuntary
   b. voluntary
   c. cerebrum

4. True or False: Nerves are made up of nerve cells called neurons.

5. True or False: An action we choose to do is called involuntary.

Answers: 1. C, 2. B, 3. A, 4. True, 5. False

ABOUT THE AUTHOR

Tracy Vonder Brink loves to learn about science and nature. She has written many nonfiction books for kids and is a contributing editor for three children's science magazines. Tracy lives in Cincinnati, Ohio with her husband, two daughters, and two rescue dogs.

Written by: Tracy Vonder Brink
Designed by: Kathy Walsh
Series Development: James Earley
Proofreader: Janine Deschenes
Educational Consultant: Marie Lemke M.Ed.

Photographs: Shutterstock; Cover: VolodymyrSanych, MDGRPHCS, graphicgeoff; p 3, 30 VolodymyrSanych; p 5, 10, 11, 13, 14, 17, 18, 21, 26 Modvector; p 4, 6, 8, 10, 12, 14, 16, 18, 20, 22, 24, 26, 28, 30 RedlineVector; p 4, 8, 10, 12, 14, 16, 18, 21, 22, 28, 32 Hluboki Dzianis; p 4 CI Photos, Luis Molinero; p 6 Magic mine, Alex Kednert; p 8 Krakenimages.com; p 9 SciePro; p 10 Terpsychore; p 11 Pracha; p 12 stockshoppe; p 13 marrishuanna; p 13 marrishuanna; p 14 gritsalak karalak; p 15 VectorMine; p 16 StockImageFactory.com; p 17 Cast Of Thousands; p 18 kurhan; p 19 polkadot_photo; p 20 K Chavan; p 21 Viacheslav Nikolaenko; p22 Kateryna Kon; p 23 BAZA Production; p 24 YAKOBCHUK VIACHESLAV; p 25 elish; p 26 pixelheadphoto digitalskillet; p 27 EDSON DE SOUZA NASCIMENTO; p 28 Prostock-studio; p 29 Ljupco Smokovski

Crabtree Publishing

crabtreebooks.com   800-387-7650
Copyright © 2023 Crabtree Publishing
All rights reserved. No part of this publication may be reproduced, stored in a retrieval system or be transmitted in any form or by any means, electronic, mechanical, photocopying, recording, or otherwise, without the prior written permission of Crabtree Publishing.

Printed in the U.S.A./012023/CG20220815

Published in Canada
Crabtree Publishing
616 Welland Ave.
St. Catharines, Ontario
L2M 5V6

Published in the United States Crabtree Publishing
347 Fifth Ave
Suite 1402-145
New York, NY 10016

Library and Archives Canada Cataloguing in Publication
Available at Library and Archives Canada

Library of Congress Cataloging-in-Publication Data
Available at the Library of Congress

Hardcover: 978-1-0398-0018-2
Paperback: 978-1-0398-0077-9
Ebook (pdf): 978-1-0398-0196-7
Epub: 978-10398-0136-3